How to Sell on Amazon: Amazon FBA, Private Labeling, Generic Selling & Reselling – The Ultimate Step by Step Guide – Make $30,000+ a Month

By Alec Brewer

Table Of Contents

Introduction   ..5

Chapter 1 – Finding a Product & Gated Categories

                                                        ..12

Chapter 2 - Retail Arbitrage   ..24

Chapter 3 – Private Labeling Vs Generic Selling   ..28

Chapter 4 – Finding a Wholesaler   ..36

Chapter 5 – Shipping Your Products   ..44

Chapter 6 – FBA (Fulfillment by Amazon) Vs FBM   ..48
(Fulfillment by Merchant)

Chapter 7– Building Your Listing   ..55

Chapter 8 – Pay Per Click & Analyzing Keywords   ..63

Chapter 9 - Marketing Private Label Products Outside
Amazon   ..71

Conclusion   ..78

Introduction

Welcome to "Make Cash Online With Amazon From Home – How to Make $30,000+ a Month on Amazon Realistically!" Do you have what it takes to make a successful online Amazon business? Can you do it? Are you ready to take action right away after reading this and build your Amazon empire? Making money online is one of the best, most relaxing ways to make money. What's better than working in the comfort of your own home, wearing your pajamas, and having no boss yelling at you? Tired of seeing your boss pulling up in a brand new BMW, while you work your butt off making minimum wage? Don't have enough money to waste your time in college? Are you sick of only getting paid on a monthly basis? There is a way to get paid everyday on Amazon! Imagine having money in your pocket everyday to live the lifestyle you've always wanted.

I wouldn't recommend quitting your job right after reading this, but instead focus more of your time towards your Amazon business. You can leave your job once you have a solid amount of money coming in every month. Since Amazon is not an instant paycheck like you are used to, you have to put in time and effort into building your business. I am telling you now, if you are looking for a get rich overnight guide, this isn't for you. You need motivation, perseverance, patience and positivity. Even though this takes hard work, this is a stupid easy way to make money compared to four years in college and thousands of hoursof boring homework. This method is far cheaper and has faster results than going through college and hopefully some day finding a decent job.

The best advice I can give you is to learn as much as you can in this book and continue to expand your knowledge beyond this. Never stop learning about new ways and techniques that could easily further your Amazon business in directions you never even knew were possible. I want you to succeed and be successful in this business! I want you to put all your maximum effort possible in this and make this business work for you. I want you to make that up to $30,000 a month or more. Heck, I want you to become a Amazon millionaire. It is possible; anything is.

I used to be a troubled kid growing up and was headed in a very bad direction. It all started in high school when I met my best friend, who was a bad influence. He introduced me to drugs and alcohol, and before I knew it I was addicted. I became a heavy stoner, drug user, and an alcoholic. I started regularly ditching class to smoke and drink. I eventually agreed to accept help from my gracious parents. Their help saved me from immersing myself further into the world or drugs and possibly ending up in jail or homeless. If I didn't have the best parents in the world, I would've been homeless long ago because who else would put up with someone who is ready to steal something any second for drugs or commit a crime. Now here I am...sober, living life, and I have worked very hard to make a complete transformation. I used to lack motivation and drive, and Iwas the laziest person. I only powered through my high school jobs because I was high on something. After becoming sober, everything changed. I realized how difficult college was and how long it would take to graduate/obtain a job. I did not want to go down that route. I also didn't want to be poor and broke working at somewhere like McDonald's for my entire life. I started listening to podcasts, watching videos and reading articles on how to start a business. When I discovered Amazon, I was so intrigued that I completely focused on learning everything I could about selling on Amazon. Why not get into a business that requires only a small investment and could potentially make me a ton of money with far less time and effort than college?

I am writing to you about what changed my life: making a Amazon business. If you want to be successful like I was, just follow everything I talk about in this ultimate guide to making big time money on Amazon. It is so important that you keep your head up and remain positive throughout all of this. Just like any business, many sellers on Amazon will encounter obstacles. When I first started, I got no sales at all. It took a week or so before I understood how to maximize pay per click to drive sales. I went through times when my supplier delayed shipments, and I ran out of stock. After running out of stock, I lost my number one spot on the search results for my product on Amazon. You have to power through all of this and know that you will succeed.

You need to have the mindset of "I can do this and I will make this work no matter what".

Many people will not support your idea to start your own Amazon business. Friends, family and coworkers might say, "oh that's silly John. Just go get a job like the rest of us."

Don't listen to average joes who are satisfied with making the same amount of money each month and a small raise every few years. That's just a sad way to make a income! Don't let negativity bring you down. Listen to people like me and countless others who have achieved success and made money on Amazon. Look up stories on the internet - you will find many people who are killing it on Amazon and fulfilling their dreams of owning their own business. Why not strive for the possibility of infinite income? Why not actually get rewarded with a higher income when you put more work into your business? It's all about what you put into a business to make it work.

If you hit a point where you are really struggling, I would recommend getting support by other solo entrepreneurs. Join a forum or facebook group for entrepreneurs or Amazon sellers.Consider hiring a mentor or motivational coach to power you through the hard times. Hopefully your family will support you like mine did. It's a big deal to have support of your family or friends. A lot of parents these days just want their kids to be college bound and don't believe in alternatives like starting a business. This is a big problem of today. Go against what others say - reach for the stars and prove everyone wrong!

Chapter 1 : Finding A Product & Gated Categories

Hey are you enjoying this book so far? If you continue reading and are liking what you read, please kindly leave a review, it would really help out as this is a brand new eBook!

The most important part of this whole entire process is finding a product to sell. Think about what kind of products interest you. Finding a product you can relate to will help you increase your ability to market it and sell it. It would be harder to sell a tennis racket and demonstrate why it's better than the competitor's tennis racket if you have no knowledge about rackets. Once you have narrowed down a few of your interests, then you can start the process of finding a product.

Before I tell you how to find the perfect product, there are some restrictions in selling in certain categories on Amazon. Amazon refers to these restricted categories as "gated," and you must meet certain requirements to sell in gated categories. Here's a list of the current

gated categories requiring approval:

Automotive & Powersports

Beauty

Clothing & Accessories

Collectible Books

Collectible Coins

Entertainment Collectibles

Fine Art

Gift Cards

Grocery & Gourmet Foods

Health & Personal Care

Independent Design

Jewelry

Luggage & Travel Accessories

Major Appliances

Services

Sexual Wellness

Shoes, Handbags & Sunglasses

Sports Collectibles

Textbook Rentals

Video, DVD, & Blu-ray

Watches

Wine

Gated categories require a professional selling plan rather than an individual one. If you are a new professional seller, you need to have a ecommerce website containing your product and brand, that can be reviewed by Amazon. Your website must include product images. You will need a recent invoice from the manufacturer that is within the last 90 days. The invoice must contain your name, contact information, company name, name of products you purchased, and name/company that sent you the invoice. Another requirement is a business license/certification that shows you registered your business in the state you are in. Additionally, you need an order defect rate of no more than 1% and a late shipment rate of no more than 4% if you are a FBM (fulfillment by merchant) seller.

Each gated category may contain additional requirements, so you'll need to review this prior to looking for a product in that area. With certain gated categories like beauty, for instance, you will also need to provide a document from the wholesaler that shows you are approved by the FDA. In the sexual wellness category, you need to have sold a minimum of 50 orders and been a registered seller on amazon for more than 90 days.

There are several resources that make finding a product much easier and provide validation so that you can make a safer decision. My favorite software, Jungle Scout, was created by Greg Mercer. Investing in the right tools is the

best thing you can do to grow a business. You will need both the Jungle Scout Web App and Google Chrome Extension. I recommend choosing month to month rather than the annual plan in the beginning to save on start up costs. Jungle Scout offers numerous filters to help you to find products. If you have no idea what you want to sell, start with the Product Database to do a more general search.

First, set the filter for the price range to $10 - $50. This is a good price range for impulse purchases. Anything under $10 will likely not be profitable after the inventory/shipping costs and Amazon fees. Many entry level sellers often look for a product that sells from $10 - $20 simply because the initial inventory costs are lower. Ideally, you should really go for a product that can sell for over $20 on Amazon. I like to aim for a net profit of at least $5 per product (after the fees Amazon takes from your listing, pay per click and inventory fees). You can set your set net price to whatever or leave it as is. Set the amount of reviews to less than 300 per month. However, I recommend choosing products that have less than 100 reviews. Products with more than 500 reviews are very competitive, and it will be difficult to be successful without a significant long-term investment in pay per click. Estimated sales should be set to at least 300 a month. This is important to assess whether the market is moving or dead. Set the number of sellers to about 5 maximum. This is important so there aren't a whole bunch of people selling the same product as you. Set the weight to a max of 1 pound. I strongly recommend finding a product that weighs no more than a pound. Shipping costs

will be outrageous if it weighs over a pound. In product tier, set the size to standard. Amazon charges additional fees for oversized items, so it's good to avoid this as a new seller. You can select different categories on the right side of your screen. I suggest focusing on one category at a time, starting with the category you're most interested in. You can also choose which marketplace for the products - stick to your country for now.

The best way to sort the results for a category is by reviews. The key is to pick a product that has low reviews, meets all the other criteria just discussed and is still making a solid amount of money each month. This way, you have a good chance of competing with other sellers and reaching the first page of the Amazon search results. You can also sort by the highest revenue to determine who is making the most money on a product and find one with low reviews.

After you find a product you're interested in by using the Jungle Scout Web App, you'll want to use the Chrome Extension tool to gather more detailed information regarding all of the sellers, daily sales, product price, etc. Go to Amazon.com and search for the product keywords. Next, click the Jungle Scout icon tool in the browser and it will show you a list of all the products. If you already know of a product you are interested in, then you can start with the Google Chrome tool. You want to check the same stats that I mentioned above. You want to look for a product selling for at $20 - $50, less than 300 reviews, preferably at least 300 sales per month, with less than 5 sellers.

Finding a product using Jungle Scout is a much easier and more reliable process. Whether you are new and have no idea what product you are looking for or you have one in mind that interests you, the software makes it simple. I am basically giving away all the steps involved to for an easy income; all you have to do is find a product. In no time at all you will have a great product to sell.

There are many successful Amazon sellers that got it right with their first product and quickly made a huge profit. Not everyone is as lucky as them. My first product was not successful for several reasons. I chose a niche product, arm chair rest covers. Even with spending $50 a day on pay per click, I wasn't getting enough sales to break even. By using the Jungle Scout Google Chrome tool, I could see that the total estimated sales for all the sellers with the same product did not reach 3000. This meant that I selected a product that was so nichy, that not enough shoppers were looking for that product each month. Initially, I disregarded this statistic because my product met all of the other criteria discussed earlier. The other issue with my product was higher than allowed returns. This occurred because it simply didn't fit enough chairs. Many customers would buy them, try them on their chair and return them. It's really important to think about finding a simple, high quality product, that has less chance of being returned. Really try to find a product with all the matching criteria I have gone over in order to try to reach that up to $30,000+ a month or more mark on Amazon.

Chapter 2: Retail Arbitrage

Another way to sell products on Amazon, is known as retail arbitrage. While some people have made significant profits doing so, I do not include this as a realistic way to make that up to $30,000+ a month or more. It is a better option if you need some temporary money, startup money, or a side job. Retail arbitrage has been increasing in popularity. Stores like Marshalls, TJ Maxx, Ross, etc sell brand name products or general products that are made by other people at a really low price compared to most places. That's why many shoppers go there for a deal. Retail arbitrage works because customers don't have access to these outlet stores or like the convenience of shopping online at home and are willing to pay full price on Amazon.

The advantage of Retail arbitrage is that you can start with a very small investment. I have heard of people being successful using only $100 to start. This is ultimately the cheapest route you can go with if you have very little money to start getting products made in China for private labeling. This is definitely a easier way to start selling on Amazon than researching a market, finding a niche, researching suppliers, designing packaging, designing logo, using/paying for pay per click, creating a listing, getting reviews, getting rank up, etc. You can look for products at discount stores like Marshalls, or you can find closeout or clearance items at stores like Walmart. There are phone apps like Amazon Price Check, that allow you to scan a barcode at the store to see what the item is selling for on Amazon. You can then determine if the item can be profitable after Amazon fees. You can use the profit from retail arbitrage to save enough money to get started in private labelling.

Retail arbitrage has some clear disadvantages, particularly as a long term plan. It is more time consuming and difficult to make a lot of money with Retail arbitrage, because you spend a lot of time hunting around for the best deals at places around town. In addition, you must constantly list all of the new items rather than focusing on listing a few private label products.

In order to reduce counterfeit products, Amazon has recently tightened up rules regarding selling certain brands. There are a number of brands you can't sell without approval from the manufacturer as a authorized reseller. You will have to become knowledgeable about what brands are restricted so you don't end up purchasing items they won't allow you to sell. Retail arbitrage can be somewhat competitive if you're selling a big brand, because there are a lot of other people trying to resell it at a lower price than the manufacture or competitors. Your margins are also going to be a lot lower then if you had your own private label business or were reselling your own products that were made in China. The biggest problem is that you will never really become rich doing retail arbitrage. I would honestly recommend working at a job and saving your money to get products made in China that are yours that you can resell for large profit margins.

Chapter 3: Private Labeling Vs Generic Selling

Once you have found a product, you need to think about the two ways you can sell that product. One way to sell a product is generically without a brand attached to it. Think of frozen pizzas like Digiorno, Totino's, and Tombstone. Walmart has their generic brand of pizza for a lower cost than the others usually. Walmart has a generic product for many big brand products at a cheaper cost. Why do people buy these generic products? Because for one, it's cheaper and usually has the same ingredients in it as the branded stuff. A generic product will cost you less to produce than a branded product with a fancy label and packaging on it. So you can offer a product for a lower cost against your competition. A lower product price gives you a better chance for higher sales and winning the buy box. It is also a lower investment because adding your logo and fancier packaging will increase the cost quite a bit. Now, generic only works best for lower priced, simple products like phone cases, phone chargers, plastic wrap, aluminum, pots, pans, etc. For these type of products, a brand name is usually not necessary for the customer to trust the product, or the price is low enough for an impulse purchase. Why wouldn't they like to save a few bucks over a brand name that's more expensive? Always make sure your generic product has the same quality or better then the brand name stuff. You can still brag about the quality in the description and bullet points. If the quality is excellent, you will have a greater chance of receiving positive reviews and less chance of returns.

When picking a brand (even if you are not placing your logo on your product), it's best to choose a generic name. If you have a brand name like "HeadphonesAAA+" people will think twice if you are selling kitchenware. Amazon has an open brand policy, so you can use one brand name to sell in multiple categories under one seller account and plan.

Unless you're 100% sure that you will be selling in one niche and category, a generic brand name allows greater flexibility. You can offer a diversity of products when you have a generic name because you can basically sell anything possible. Using a great sounding name like "TopDeals4U," for instance, could apply to many different products and categories. See how that sounds amazing and also provides the shopper with the feeling that you offer the best deals on the market! You will get a ton of buyers if your name has a strong marketing pull in it.

There's always a small chance that a generic brand name might make people think that they are not getting as high of quality as a product as a competitor with a brand name suited for that exact product. However, you can counter this by making sure your product quality is on point. Customer satisfaction comes down to what people think when they use your product, and how it compares in quality, bang for the buck, and ease of use.

The other way of selling products is known as private labeling. What is it exactly? Private labeling is when you create your own brand and slap it on products that are made for you. Think of Nike and how they make shoes, shirts, hoodies, etc. They place their Nike logo on products to so people know that is made by the Nike brand. While definitely more expensive, placing your logo on the item gives it a more professional look. Private labeling can really go a long way as far as the marketing you can do and building your brand. Of course, you can just create a brand, make a website and sell it on Amazon, but there is always more you can do.

If you want to go the extra mile, you can make a professional looking website or hire someone to do it for you. You can direct traffic to your Amazon product link. Driving sales to Amazon will get you to page one in the search results quicker since Amazon places sellers higher up that have greater sales. You can have your own web store and direct customers to just buy on your site. I would recommend you do both, so you can sell orders on both your website and Amazon. It's always a good plan not to rely strictly on Amazon for your sales. If you can build a business off of Amazon as well, it increases your security in case anything happens with Amazon.

Before getting into how to market your private label brand for Amazon, lets talk about the advantages of private labeling, disadvantages, and more about it. You first need to find a wholesaler, which is what we talk about in the next chapter. The wholesaler needs to be able to do private labeling services. Most wholesale suppliers can brand your logo on the product or packaging. Usually when you ask suppliers for private labeling services, there is a bigger upfront cost rather than just buying generic wholesale products. Because they are doing this special service for you, they are going to have a certain minimum order quantity requirement that will most likely be higher than if you were to just order a generic products.

Depending on the product, you will need an investment of at least $500 to a couple thousand dollars. It depends on how much faith you have in the product you picked out. I do think you should start out with a generic product just to minimize the start up costs and learn the whole process of selling a product on Amazon. If your generic product starts selling well, consider adding the logo. A well designed logo and packaging will allow you to sell it for more money and distinguish your product from competitors. There is no question that a private label product will increase your sales and make more money than a generic product would.

One thing you need to think about is that you need to have a logo design ready in a specific format for the suppliers on Alibaba in order for them to provide an estimate. You don't need to possess the creativity of an artist or designer to make a custom product box and cover. Always look online for other ideas and at your competition on Amazon. I recommend using some type of online product maker or Photoshop if you are good at it. You can also easily hire someone to do it for you on sites like Fiverr. Just make sure it's someone that has referrals or positive feedback. People love a modern and clean looking packaging design, and it

will really stand out against other products. People will pay that extra few dollars just because of how professional your products look like compared to others.

While it's not mandatory to have a web site if you are selling on Amazon, I highly recommend building one. Customers on Amazon will sometimes check out your site for more information if they are unfamiliar with your brand. Should you choose to apply for brand registration with Amazon, you will be required to have a website displaying your products. You can make a basic site that meets the minimum requirements such as your phone number, email, brand name, and address on it, but I don't recommend that. Think outside the box. Amazon marketplace does all the advertising for you, especially when you use pay per click, but why not go further than that? Why not grow your brand and make more money? Making a really professional looking site is not that difficult or expensive. You can even make a free site, but it will typically have limited features as well as the company's name in the URL link. There are many affordable solutions that start at only a few dollars a month. I recommend companies like Freewebstore, Wix or Strikingly as the best simple, low-cost site builders. The more time and effort you put into this, the better the results are going to be. Don't be afraid to learn - it is so easy to use a website maker software like this. It's not as confusing and intimidating as it may sound. If you really can't get a hold of it, you can add to the fees and hire someone to make you a professional clean looking website.

Chapter 4 : Finding a Wholesaler

So far, I've covered how to find a product to sell on Amazon using software. Whether you are a new seller or experienced, this guide can help you. Have found a product that looks good and meets all the requirements I mentioned? If the answer is yes, you are ready for the next step. Let me teach you how to source your product from a wholesaler.

The best place to source a wholesaler for your product is Alibaba. You can also try AliExpress. AliExpress is similar, but it is not meant to really buy in bulk, and the quality is not always as good. Aliexpress is a good site for those who have less money to invest or to test a product on Amazon

Alibaba is the main source for wholesale items outside the U.S. This is the best place on the internet to get a good deal and quality. They also offer protection for buyers if you purchase through their site. You can try to find wholesale companies or manufacturers in made in your country, but the cost per unit will always be higher and the minimum order quantity tends to be higher as well. The nice thing, though, is that you get to tell people your products are made in the USA, which can be comforting to a lot of buyers. The shipping will of course be a lot less than from China to you.

When searching for an item, start with being specific. Alibaba search results will display pages and pages of items, you need to be specific on exactly what you want for your product. If I was looking for a "enamel steel camping mug," I wouldn't type in "mug or cup." I start with typing in "enamel steel camping mug or enamel steel mug." Make sure you always get a sample of the product before purchasing a real order. Once you have found your item you want to check for trade assurance in the search terms. This ensures your orders are protected until the item is safely delivered. If you choose to pay a supplier directly without trade assurance, there's no protection if you never receive the item. The next thing you want to check is for a gold supplier. This shows that the supplier has good history and feedback through Alibaba and has met certain criteria, including third party verification. You can also view the company's established year to see how long they have been selling on Alibaba.

Under the title of the product the USD price per unit. This varies in price for a reason. Basically, the larger you buy the cheaper, it is per item. The smaller you buy, the more expensive each item is. I recommend starting with a smaller order. This is a test run for you to see if the item can sell, of customers are happy with the quality, etc. Start with 100 units and see how well they sell. The pieces amount of minimum pieces or order quantity is located under the price. Some suppliers will have a high minimum order quantity, but if you're truly interested in this item, you can message the supplier. The best approach is to ask them to lower the minimum order quantity it so you can do a test run. This has worked for me before actually just by sending them a message.

Let's talk about how to properly talk to a supplier on Alibaba and how to ask all the right questions so that there is no confusion. First, introduce yourself and talk as if you're a representative from a company. Say something like "Hi, (name here) how are you doing today? We are very interested in your product and would like to ask a few questions. Is your product high quality? Would you be willing to offer a sample of (the exact product and model(s)) to this area code in the US? How much would this cost for a sample including shipping? How long would the sample take to arrive? Could we brand our logo and make custom packaging for the product if available (only if you are doing private labeling)? Do you take Alipay or PayPal? What is your minimum order requirement for this product? Thank you so much for your time we look forward to talking with you!"

Let me explain the purpose of the questions mentioned and the reasoning behind them. Asking them how they are doing today will demonstrate to them that you are showing respect and care about their lives, not just doing business. It is important to be very respectful when speaking with the Chinese suppliers. They have a very friendly culture, and they value building a solid relationship. This could be your potential supplier for the product that could make $10,000+ a month on Amazon! It is so very important to build a strong relationship with them. Don't be afraid to get a little personal, but again keep it professional. Send them a nice greeting and show them that you care about them. Telling them you are very interested in there product shows that you are a serious buyer. Asking them if there product is high quality is a good idea because they may offer multiple kinds of that product of different quality. For example, the magnets I used to sell came in three different kinds of magnetism. Each one was in a different magnetic strength, the highest ensuring the most magnetism to any object such as metal, fridges, cars, etc. I wanted to get the best quality and the magnetism that had the highest power so everyday materials would magnetize to it without a problem. I wanted to beat my competitors with a better product. I did have a very high quality product at almost only two dollars a product to buy it wholesale. It was very profitable, even after Amazon FBA and pay per click fees.

Asking about a sample is critical before you purchase a real order. It would be terrible to spend a lot of money and receive products that are broken, don't work, and are cheap low quality. You need to test the quality in order to assure your order will be sell-able. Always ask for a sample and include your zip code so they can calculate how much the shipping will be. Usually the sample is free, you just have to pay the somewhat large shipping fee. The sample fee usually costs around $50, but it is worth it to ensure you get a high quality product. I have received many samples that I chose not to order due to poor quality, lack of features or functionality. Ask them how long it will take for the sample to arrive. In my experience, samples take about a week to two weeks at most, which is super fast coming from another country.

If you are going to private label, always inquire whether you can send them a logo to use and if they can make custom packaging. Ask how much extra it will cost for private labeling. Make sure they accept Alipay or PayPal for the sample or first order. These are very safe ways to pay to prevent getting scammed. If they only do bank wire transfer or something where you cannot get your money back (no trade assurance through Alibaba), find another supplier. They may not be a scammer, but why take that risk of losing your hard earned money? In the future, many suppliers will ask you to pay directly through bank wire without trade assurance. This is often done because they are bypassing the fees charged by Alibaba and thus able to give you a better deal. You may choose to consider this in the future once you have developed a relationship and trust.

Although the minimum order requirement is often displayed on product listing, it is sometimes flexible as mentioned before. If the order quantity is too high, many suppliers will work with you if you state that it's a test order. Remember to start out small to test the waters. Finally, thanking them and telling them you look forward to doing business is not only professional, but is also a common courtesy.

Chapter 5 : Shipping

There are a few different options available to ship products from the supplier. The first way is door to delivery by express air. This is the quickest way to receive goods and also the most expensive option. Once the products are ready to ship, It can take a week or two for the cargo to arrive at your warehouse or house. For small shipments and new sellers, door to door delivery via express air is the best option. Despite it being more expensive, I have always personally selected air freight express, because it reduces stress and complications. Everyone wants things to be easier right? As with all shipping methods, the price of air express depends on the weight of the products. An example of pricing for one of my products was about $500 for 500 pieces. The air freight express shipping was approximately $1,000. As you can see, the cost to ship was twice the price of the actual product, hence the need to choose a light product. Keep in mind this key: find the lowest weight product with the highest selling price on Amazon to get the highest profit margins. This is really the most valuable key information I can give you. You can also speak to the supplier about getting your shipment sent straight to Amazon, which may slightly reduce your time and costs (only if you are are doing FBA). We will talk about that in the next chapter.

I want to share a little experience and add something very important about air freight express shipping. One mistake I made early on caused a huge headache, financial loss and delay of receiving my goods. When you speak to the supplier, be very clear that you want "door to door" shipping, and confirm that you want it sent to your house or warehouse and not just to the airport. Make sure that the invoice you receive specifies in writing "door to door." Suppliers will sometimes offer a cheaper option of shipping to the airport, and you must deal with the rest. This occurred once due to a miscommunication with a seller that we had previously dealt with. Our products were shipped in on a plane and left at the airport. No one could locate the products. My partners and I called tons of places and no one could find the cargo. Normally, if you select door to door delivery, the supplier chooses FedEx, UPS or DHL. Those companies are experts in clearing customs and moving the packages through quickly. If cargo is just left at the airport, not only are you responsible for transporting it, but you also have to clear customs. Clearing customs is complicated and often involves hiring a customs broker to complete the paperwork and get the goods released to you. There are fees owed to customs and to the customs broker. Ultimately, this mistake cost an extra $500 to resolve with all of the fees and ended up being far costlier than shipping door to door.

The second way to get your goods delivered is by sea freight. This basically means that your goods will be sent on a cargo like ship, and it will generally take one to two months for them to arrive in the United States and clear customs. This is a great way to cut costs if you are buying a massive amount of products. Sea freight can cost up to 50% less than door to door delivery via air with huge shipments. The reason you don't use this shipping method when you are buying a low amount of products is because there a lot of fees involved here, and it is only cost effective for larger shipments. Shipping by sea is far more complicated, so you will need to hire a freight forwarding company to handle the goods for you. There is far more documentation required, and many fees, duties, licenses, taxes, etc. when shipping by sea. Many freight forwarding companies also provide customs brokerage services. If they do not offer customs broker services, you will need to to hire a customs broker. It will be a much smoother process if you choose a freight forwarder that does both. You can find freight forwarders online. It is best to contact several freight forwarders with your information (number of products, weight, location, etc) to get quotes. Shipping by sea is a great option to use when you have a lot more knowledge and are further in your career of Amazon selling.

Chapter 6 : FBA (Fulfillment by Amazon) vs FBM (Fulfillment by Merchant)

We have covered how to properly find a product and examine it, making sure it's the best it can be. We have talked about figuring out the best tactics on finding the right wholesaler on Alibaba for your Amazon product. Finally, we have talked about the ways to get your products shipped to you. So, let's dive into the differences between FBA and Fulfillment by Merchant. In my opinion, the best way to sell your products and have them shipped to customers is by FBA. This means fulfillment by Amazon. You send your products directly to some of Amazon's warehouses, and they ship each product to the customer when an order is placed. Why is this better? Amazon takes all the headaches away of packing individual orders and getting them shipped out quickly. If you pack your own orders, you would be limited to the amount of packages you could physically handle packing and shipping daily. Furthermore, Amazon takes responsibility for shipping deadlines and delays, so if something happens, your seller metrics aren't affected. Amazon holds sellers to shipping deadlines, and even delays caused by USPS, FedEx, etc., that aren't your fault will negatively affect your seller metrics. They handle the majority of customer service issues, unless a customer directly messages you. They also handle returns for FBA.

To ship FBA, you have to make sure you follow the directions to pack your products in the right way to be prepared for FBA. Amazon has tight restrictions on the way the want the products. If you do not follow Amazon rules regarding preparing and shipping your products, they won't accept your products for FBA and will send them back. All products must have a scannable bar code on the outside of the packaging. They do not accept products that require Amazon employees to assemble things. They will not accept loose items; everything must be wrapped or packaged in something. If you are selling a bundle or set of something on Amazon, it must be shrink wrapped, placed in a clear bag, or a box and marked with a sold as a set sticker. If the box has openings or perforated sides, it has to pass a drop test of about 3 feet or so. Poly bags that have a 5" opening or larger are required to have a suffocation warning on them. You can actually purchase poly bags with a suffocation warning on them from Amazon to help you out and prevent any mishaps. The thickness of your bag must be at least 1.5 mils at least. The polybag must be transparent and completely sealed, and the poly bag can not extend more than 3" past the product. Case packed products need to have a matching SKU. All the boxes with the same product also need to have the same amount of products in each of the boxes. The case limit is 150 units per case to be exact. For food items and such, you need expiration dates on the master carton in a 36 point font and on each of the individual products as well. It must go by month-day-year. These are just some examples of the basic preparation guidelines. Amazon has a help section and instructional videos within your Seller Central account to teach you how to prepare your and ship your items. The requirements can change, so it's best to periodically check your account to see if anything has changed. You can also search "Amazon FBA packing requirements" online to find specific information.

I recommend doing FBA if you are even just starting out. It takes a lot of time away of having to do things manually and constantly running to the post office, UPS, or FEDEX. Shipping from your home or warehouse to Amazon is affordable - you get huge discounts through UPS, FedEx, etc. as an FBA seller. The prices for Amazon Warehouses to store the inventory are not expensive, especially if the products are small and lightweight. FBA gives you a chance to win the buy-box easier as well. It gives you a lot of free time to work on your Amazon listing, pay per click, and more. There are a few cons to FBA. One is that the FBA fee is higher than if you were FBM. For example, on one of my items priced at $24.99, the total Amazon fees are $6.74. The great part is that you can see the Amazon fee estimate when you create the listing, so you'll know exactly what will be deducted. The FBA fee covers Amazon managing the inventory, packing the individual order, shipping it out, customer service, and handling returns, so I personally feel it's worth it. I started FBA right away for my products because I did not want to deal with the headache of sending each product to someone in the mail. Another disadvantage is long term storage fees if your items don't sell quickly. You can avoid this by starting out with smaller shipments or removing items that don't sell.

FBM shipping is fulfillment by the merchant. This means for every order you receive, you have to manually ship each item to the customer. You are responsible for handling customer service in a timely manner (responding to emails within 24 hours) as well as all returns. A plus to FBM is that you maintain control of your entire product inventory. It is easier for it not to get lost or misplaced, as can sometimes happen in Amazon's warehouses. Storage fees can be lower as well, particularly with large, bulky items. If Amazon stores the item in their warehouse, the larger the item, the more expensive the storage fees will be. Generally, FBM is better suitable for those selling very large items, or for large companies with a warehouse team in place to quickly fulfill orders. With FBM, you can now participate in Seller Fulfilled Prime. This is great because you can entice buyers with fast, free shipping. You have to meet very strict standards though in order to participate in the prime program and remain in good standing with Amazon. Keep in mind that choosing FBM means you need to be extremely motivated and not miss a shipment or do a late shipment. You can get penalized for this and eventually get kicked off of Amazon. Missing or late shipments can also lower your seller rating. The seller rating affects how you show up in Amazon searches and reduces your chances of selling more, giving the competitor the advantage to outperform you. FBA sellers usually have the advantage in winning the buy box, so to compete you might have to lower your price. This could start a pricing war and then no one makes money. Generally, I would simply go with FBA rather than FBM unless you are selling large, bulky items, slow-moving items that could incur long-term storage fees, certain seasonal items and large companies with their own warehouses. Take out the headaches, there is already enough to worry about besides the shipping portion of Amazon.

Chapter 7 : Building Your Listing

What is the secret to building the best listing for Amazon once your products are ready to go? The first thing we are going to talk about is the title for your product. Most categories have a 250 character limit for the title. Next to the product picture, the title is the most important thing that shoppers are going to see right away. Try to think about what people most want to know about your product that will make them want to click on your listing. In addition, try to place something in the title that sets your listing apart from the competitor. Place the most important keywords in the beginning of your title. Include your brand name if you have one. You might want to include your brand name at the end because people aren't going to search for your brand if it is not well known, and it's likely not the most important aspect of your product that will grab them. Include the color, flavor, or type of product it is. Always include the size or units it comes with, for example "(Set of 1)." Capitalize the first letter of each word. Spell out measurements like cups or ounces. Likewise, spell out units in the product (e.g. put "100 pieces" rather than 100 pcs."). Do not spell numbers like six, but instead use the numeric form of "6". It is best to use "&" instead of "and". The word "and" is not significant so make it less apparent as possible, and don't waste the limited characters allowed on it. Here is what not to include in your Amazon product listing title. Do not include the price, words in all caps, seller info, promotions, words like best or #1, symbols, size if it's not related to the product, and color if the product doesn't come in other colors.

Next is the "Key Products Feature" in the description section. This is essentially the bullet point section at the top of Amazon listings, near the product image. You should have 5 or more bullet points in your listing. Make sure you use all of them. Do not just put two bullets - this is your chance to make your product shine and distinguish your product from the competition. The first thing to do is research your competitor's listings to get an idea of what they are highlighting. See how to make your points better than theirs. Next, look at your competitors reviews to determine what made customers like it enough to give a 5 star review. This gives you a good basis to determine what matters most to your customers. Look at negative reviews to see what customers disliked. If your product is better or different, highlight that as a key benefit. Always list the most important benefits at the top and the less critical features toward the bottom. Each bullet listing has about a 500 character limit, so do not be afraid to really fill these suckers with relevant keywords. Remember that repeating the same keywords is not helpful on Amazon. Make sure the bullet points flow well and are readable. It is okay to write in fragments since these are bullet points. Make sure that spelling, grammar and punctuation is correct. Include things like color, shape, and material of the product. You might want to say like "Made in the USA" or "Highest quality of materials." Use words that pop out to the reader and differ from competitors. Try to make the bullets as long as you possibly can without sacrificing quality and readability. Amazon will use the keywords in this section to rank you higher in the search results of your product. Bad examples would be a bullet like "Satisfaction Guaranteed" or "Top Quality." You want to include those, but as part of a longer bullet point.

The next part of the listing is the "Description" of your Amazon listing. The description needs to be really specific about your product. Like the other sections, refer back to competitors reviews and their description. If you see the same kind of features and benefits repeatedly listed in their product descriptions, isn't that boring to you? It will also appear boring to customers. You need to think of how to make your listing stand out from other listings in the game. Use points that demonstrate how your product is better than the rest and what makes it better than other competitors. Do not just talk about the basics; think of selling points other listings don't contain. It is very important to use your target keywords, but do not stuff keywords and make it difficult or confusing to read. Some of you may be familiar with keyword stuffing in reference to Google, but in Amazon, keyword stuffing doesn't help your listing at all. As mentioned earlier, the location of your keyword matters, and the most important keywords should be located in the front. Include similar and alternative words that you think people would search for and want in a product. Now, let's look at an example of a great description. The product is a pair of headphones, and we'll make up a brand name like Kronic In Ear Headphones. Here is an example of a poor description : The Kronic In Ear Headphones have good bass, good mids, and are good quality headphones. That sounds boring, right? Instead a better description would be : The Kronic In Ear Headphones are the absolute best in ear headphone ear buds on the market! They have heart pounding, shaking bass that will rattle your brain! They have clear and crisp clean vocal quality to allow you to listen to every part of your favorite song. See how I included good relevant keywords, illustrated the benefits and pumped up the listing with powerful words. This is what you want to do to your listing. Pump the readers up, tell a story with your description, and make them look at something different the rest of the competing products on the market of Amazon.

Now let's talk about your photos. Your photo is perhaps the most important part of your listing, and the first thing that will grab the customer's attention. If the picture is poor quality, the customer will probably not click on the listing, especially if you have competitors that use good photos. The first product image shown is the most important picture and first impression of your product. There are a number of options for getting great product photos. You can take your own photos. Make sure you use a high quality camera or high quality phone camera. The first product image should show your product clearly on a white background. You can not include watermarks or additional graphics/text. While you may see some sellers include these things, it's a violation of the rules and not something you want to risk. You can buy a photo light booth (available on Amazon, of course), use a piece of white posterboard or even take the picture and edit it in Photoshop to achieve a white background. There are numerous apps and filters on your phone that can also improve the clarity or lighting of your photo. If you do not want to take the picture yourself, you can pay someone to take product photos for you. Look online or for a local photographer that has experience with product photography. With a little effort, you can really produce nice photos at home. I recommend just doing it yourself, particularly in the beginning to save on start up expenses. Make sure you follow Amazon's rules to make your product pictures 1000 pixels or bigger in height or width. This will let people zoom in on your photo so they can see the details. Make sure the product is in perfect condition with no scratches, scuffs, or loose parts hanging.

Drawings of the product are not allowed; only the physical product can be included in the product images. Try to make the product in the picture look as large as possible so in the search results it shows up really big and bright compared to others. You want also include lifestyle pictures of a model or someone using the product and its functions. For example, I used to sell magnets that stick to the wall. I included pictures of things that would stick to the magnets in a garage or kitchen setting for example. Show the viewers ways product can be used and how easy it is to use. Amazon will allow about 9 images maximum on your listing. Try to include as many images as possible, because that increases the likelihood that the customer will click on your listing, and it's a powerful visual sales tool.

Chapter 8: Pay Per Click & Analyzing Keywords

We are almost finished with this tutorial and now on to what I think are the top secrets to making $10,000 a month on Amazon. One of the most powerful ways to launch your product and get sales is by advertising on Amazon. This is optional but highly recommended for increased sales and visibility. Just like Google, Facebook, etc., Amazon has their own paid for of advertisement referred to as Pay Per Click. You will be setting up Pay Per Click advertising through your Amazon seller central account. I am going to teach and explain the steps to building the proper pay per click campaign. We will start with how to structure the first two weeks after product launch and then discuss how to adjust from there.

Let's get right into it. You will need to invest quite a bit of money the first two weeks of your Pay Per Click campaign. You need to start with a high budget of pay per click each day to see any results and to determine what keywords to use. It is recommended that you start out with a daily budget of $50 for your first two weeks using a manual campaign. An auto campaign is technically for beginners. Amazon chooses the keywords they think are relevant to your listing, and you are supposed to use this information to discover the best keywords. However, the keywords tend to less accurate, and you will likely waste more money compared to picking your own keywords with a manual campaign. In my first manual campaign, I quickly got up to over 20 orders per day to be exact. A manual campaign means that you choose the keywords you want to bid for pay per click. It's really not difficult to guess what keywords are important to your product. Look on Amazon and see what competitors are using for keywords in their product such as titles, description, etc. Think of the most common references for them. You can also try this free keyword tool for Amazon: https://keywordtool.io/amazon. Type in your exact product name and it will show many other names and what people search for. I recommend you start with at least 20 keywords in your manual campaign, even though Amazon recommends 100. Just try to pick as many keywords you possibly can that are related to your product type and name and set them to a "broad match." Broad match will allow your ad to display when the keyword or related keywords are searched for. This will show you what keyword works best and other search terms that customers are using. On each keyword, you should bid at least $2 - $3 to start with. If you start with a low amount and your competitors outbid you, your ad either won't display or it will display further into the search results. Since the goal is really to reach page 1, it's important to invest in high bids that will get you there. Keep in mind that Amazon won't automatically charge you the $2 - $3 max you bid on. You'll be charged up to that amount, only if your competitors are bidding high.

Do your manual campaign and wait two weeks to analyze it by looking at the search term report. The search term reports are located in the Reports section of your seller central admin. Download the report, and export it to a program like Microsoft Excel, Numbers on Mac, etc so you can analyze it in an easier form. There are extra fields that aren't critical, so just delete those so it's less confusing to view. The most critical fields to keep are the Customer Search Term, Keyword, Impressions, Clicks, CTR, Total Spent, ACoS, Orders, and Conversion Rate. You want to focus on what keyword has the highest impressions, clicks, and orders placed within the week. The ACoS field tells you how much the sale cost to get. Keywords that have a high ACoS rate means that you are spending too much money to get the sale and will most likely lose money. You need to lower bids on words that have a high ACoS rate. If the ACoS rate is low that means you are making money on it, and it's doing well. Try to strive for an ACoS rate under 20% or so. For example an ACoS rate of 15% would mean you are making sales of around $15,000 and spending only $2,000 or so. That is a very good turn around rate. When I looked at my report for the first time after launching my auto campaign for two weeks, the keywords were a bunch of random numbers. This means customers found your product by looking for your ASIN or they found your product through another competitors product's page. This won't happen when you pick a manual campaign with your own keywords. See what keywords are working and eliminate those that aren't. By using broad match keywords, you will discover other search terms customers are using so you can focus on those. You can move keywords into phrase or exact match once you are getting a lost of sales on them.

Move poor performing keywords into the negative campaign so that your ad will not display if the customer types in those keywords. I recommend continuing to spend $50 a day or however much you can afford to spend for this manual campaign. You need to get your product in front of customers. When you start getting sales from Pay Per Click, your organic sales will also increase. This is because Amazon will place you higher in the search results and closer to page one as your sales increase. If you want to decrease your advertising expenses, wait until you are consistently getting a lot of orders each day. You can then start experimenting with reducing the daily pay per click expense by $5 every two weeks or so to ensure that your sales don't drastically decrease. Don't mess with your pay per click per campaign, though, if you are seeing that you are spending a small amount on pay per click and your sales are sky high. The ultimate goal is to get to a point where you don't need pay per click at all. However, you will most likely always need it unless you are far above your competitors in rank, reviews, sales, etc. Many categories and products are so competitive that you must continue to do pay per click because your competitors are.

I started out with $50 a day and in no time was on the first page in sponsored for Amazon. Amazon will reward you for spending money with them as they did with me. I even got the title "#1 New Seller" in new products for my category. If you cannot spend $50 per day, even something like $25 will help. You will see slower results, but you will still see results. By using Pay Per Click, you should expect sales pretty quickly within a few days. If you aren't seeing results,

it could be that you're not spending enough or you need to evaluate your product picture and title to make sure that the problem doesn't lie with your listing. If you're getting a lot of impressions but not a lot of click throughs (CTR), it could be your listing. If your impressions are low, you need to increase the bid. I have known people that start with spending $100 a day on pay per click. If you have the extra money, the only thing it can do it most likely make you on page 1 at the top of the page. It can only convert to higher sales. Only do that if you really have the money to blow. Do not expect to break even right away or even make any money. Very few people will get that lucky right away honestly. Expect a few months to elapse before you start seeing yourself break even or making money. Your business is an investment. This is not a get rich overnight guide; everything takes time and effort.

Chapter 9: Marketing Private Label Products Outside Amazon

How can you market your private label business on a budget? First, you need to know your product. You might have to do some research on the kind of products you are selling. Your supplier's listing on Alibaba will often provide you with many of the key features. It's also a good idea to look at competitors with similar products on Amazon. See what type of benefits and features they mention. You can use tons of free social networking websites such as Facebook, Instagram, and Twitter. To make this work you really need to step outside of your comfort zone in order to see results. Shake some hands, talk to people, and get to know them. Don't be afraid of what others will think of you. It's all about the money, making it, and seeing the results.

There will always be people that think you are silly or are a waste of time - just ignore them. It's important to maintain positive energy and keep your head up high. You need to be confident that your business will work and succeed. Think that this will all pay off in a matter of time. It may be weeks, months, or a year, but you will see results eventually if you are persistent and determined.

There is this great site called helpareporter.com, where people are looking for a new story to put out for news or major media places. If you can create a story about your how your product is very innovative or the hot new thing, maybe your story will be selected and released. One of the best ways is to give away your product as a free trial or for free. This will allow users to experience the product and spread word to friends, family, co-workers, etc. Another good marketing strategy is have you ever seen sites that list top gifts for co-workers or inexpensive secret Santa gift ideas? I recommend contacting these sites and asking them to show your product as a idea. This could drive a ton of traffic to your Amazon listing or website.

Email marketing and building an email list is an important and effective way to grow your Amazon business as well as business via your web site. Developing an email list can help when launching a new product on Amazon. To build your email list, target people via social media or paid social media marketing on Instagram or Facebook. Set up some automated email campaigns that can be sent to people to increase your sales and traffic. You can offer shoppers incentives, promotions, etc to them. If you can find out what customers had your product in their cart, but didn't buy it, send them a email! Find out why they didn't buy your product and use that knowledge to better learn how to improve your product, listing, website, etc.

Another great way to grow your private label business is to start an affiliate program. People will get a small commission if someone clicks on your product and purchases it because they came from a link from the affiliate. This works by creating a custom URL link for each person that promotes or sells your product. They can easily share this in a blog, social media, etc causing even more traffic and exposure to your product! You need to get free press if you can for your private label business.

There are many bloggers out there. Look for blogger web sites and bloggers on social media. Contact them about your product and get them to post a blog about it. Offer them a free product for them to review as well as an affiliate link so that they can get a commission if their subscribers purchases. You can also start your own blog or find ways to post your blogs to mainstream channels. Web site builders like Strikingly make it simple to start your own blog. For more information about this, type into Google, "hacking the press clever ways to get free press coverage."

I would also recommend making a YouTube channel to show your product and how it works. The whole point of this is to get your product and brand out there. Every effort of something will help in some way. There are ways to promote your YouTube video as well, which is a huge subject in itself. Make sure to use good keywords as well as detailed/accurate titles and descriptions of your video. Use good tags that are relevant to your product. Encourage people to like, share, and subscribe to your video. Use your video on your website and put a link to the video in your blogs or blogs that people write for you. Having a video that demonstrates your products and benefits is extremely powerful.

Back to marketing your private labeling business. You can go live with a fairly new program called Periscope. Lots of people are already using this to promote themselves and get traffic. It is basically a live broadcast of you. Show a demo of your product, how it works, functions, etc. Pinterest is another free way to promote or display your products that have a great look or cool feature.

Facebook is one of the most powerful ways to market your business. Everyone uses facebook, right? Facebook now has over 2 billion monthly users. You can create a business fan page that is attached to your personal account, where you can post information about your product and promotions or sales. If your product falls in a niche, you can create a facebook group by posting information, news, pictures and things of interest to people in this niche. Facebook ads are one of the best paid forms of advertisement today. I recommend this if you a little money to spare. These ads tend to be very good because you know basically who you are targeting. Facebook ads has developed an excellent system of targeting very specific groups of people. You can select the age, part of the country, interests, etc. You can select people who follow certain similar brands. I recommend spending at least $5/day and running a promotion for your product. If you can source your product for a small amount of money, you can offer a free plus shipping promotion. Your ad will say that the item is free for a limited time if they just pay shipping. You'll charge enough for shipping to cover both shipping and the product cost. If you're product is cheap and light enough, you can earn a profit as well. This is a great way to build your email list, gain a new customer to market to and possibly upsell once they click on your ad. Whatever type of promotion you choose to run, make sure it is valuable enough to grab their attention.

There are even more ways to market your business, but I've briefly touched on the most important ones. If you really want to earn that $10,000+ a month, you'll want to spend all your time on marketing your product and brand. How hard are you willing to work? What kind of effort are you going to put in? How are you going to make this work?

Conclusion

Congratulations! If you made it to this part of my book, that means you had the motivation to read and finish it. Soak in all the information. I encourage you to take notes about everything important and key points for each chapter. Let's go over what we have talked about, particularly the most important points. We talked about how to find the best product and all the filters on Jungle Scout to use. We talked over the best criteria to make sure a product is the best to sell on Amazon, which is so important - I cannot stress that enough. Pick a product that sells for more than $20, weighs less than 1 pound, has less than 100 reviews and 5 sellers. We discussed avoiding gated categories in the beginning and which categories are better. Again, the best categories too look for products in are books, beauty, health, home, garden, luggage/travel accessories, sexual wellness, toys, baby, industrial, and sports/outdoors. We have explored how you can resell products from valid outlets and do what's called retail arbitrage on Amazon. This isn't a route to get rich or earn that up to $30,000+ a month or more, it is just a way to get temporary money or startup money. In Chapter 3, we talked about the positives and negatives of private labeling vs generic selling, and also how to market your private labeling business besides just pay per click. Remember going that extra mile will you bring you closer to earning up to $30,000+ a month or more on Amazon. It's all about how much work you are willing to put it into your business to make that big money. Show the consumers that your generic product is just the same quality as the brand name ones. A brand name is specific to a certain product and a generic name can be used for almost everything. Private labeling is going to be more expensive and time consuming, but it's ultimately a bigger payoff than a generic product. In Chapter 4, we talked about wholesaling and how to find the best wholesaler for your Amazon product. Alibaba is the leading place to find a product, while you can use AliExpress for small orders or samples. It's important to always get a sample of the product before purchasing a big or small order even. Make sure you check the boxes for trade assurance and gold supplier on Alibaba. We talked about how to talk properly to the Chinese suppliers because they have a culture of showing respect and developing relationships. Only do bank wires or transfers when you have done a few orders with them and can trust them. In Chapter 5, we discussed how to get the goods from China shipped to you. The fastest way, and the best way for new sellers is to receive items by express air. Make sure the invoice clearly states that shipping is door to door. The second method is sea freight shipping, which is only recommended for large shipments and when you have time to wait for the products. Remember sea freight shipping works best when you are further along in your Amazon career and need to order a huge amount of stock. In Chapter 6, we learned about FBA (fulfillment by Amazon) vs FBM (fulfillment by merchant). The easiest way is FBA. This means Amazon takes care of customer service and sending your products out to customers. I recommend this method even if you are just starting out because there are so many other important things to worry about beyond just getting your products shipped out to customers. In Chapter 7, we talked about how to build the proper listing to give you an advantage over other listings on Amazon. The first important piece is the title. The most important keywords should always be in the front. Include the type of product it is, color, flavor, size, etc. and your brand name if you have one. Do not include price, words in all caps, seller info, promotions, words like best or #1, symbols, size if it's not related to the product, and color if the product doesn't come in other colors. Check what people liked and complained about on competitor's products, and use that to your advantage, so you can show how your product is better. Stand out from other listings with something different. Include keywords, but don't stuff the same words. Use important, relevant keywords in your description and bullet points. Make sure you use all 5 of your bullet points and that it is easy for customers to read. Start with the most important information and as you go down use the less important stuff. Include things like color, shape, material, benefits, etc. Use a high quality camera for your photos, making sure the first image is on a white background with no additional text or graphics. Include lifestyle photos that show how easy the product is to use. Chapter 8 covered Pay Per Click marketing on Amazon and how to use/analyze it. Pay Per Click is very important when you start. It will be hard to successfully launch your product without it. Start out with a $50 daily budget on a manual campaign, bid $2 to $3 on keywords, and analyze the data at 2 weeks. This will make your ranking increase significantly and make you show up a lot easier without it. Try to keep your ACoS rate low (around 20%). A high ACoS rate means you are losing money. The point is to adjust your campaigns and the bid on keywords to get to a point where you are making money and lowering the pay per click cost maybe each week. I recommend you continue with the $50, $100 or however much you can spend if you want to keep those sales high on Amazon. Chapter 9 touched on marketing ideas beyond Amazon. You can market your private labeling brand with your website, social media, email marketing, ads, word of mouth, making cards, getting it out to a reporter, contacting other businesses, affiliate marketing, bloggers/blogging, etc.

We have now thoroughly covered everything in every chapter of my eBook. I believe you can truly succeed if you if you put in the effort and work and follow the steps in this book. You can start on your second product at any time you are ready. However, I would recommend waiting until your first product has a good, stable track record for a few months. Wait until you have perfected pay per click and your campaign is pretty much flawless with the right numbers.

Also, invite customers to review your product for every sale you get it. Their Amazon email address will display in your orders. Amazon now allows customers to unsubscribe from emails, so you will need to keep track of this if Amazon notifies you that the message can't be delivered for this reason. There are some services that you can auto send email campaigns to customers as well. This works by it automatic sending an email when the customer has bought the item, before shipment, after shipment, etc.

There are many sellers making millions on Amazon - just look at some of the top selling products on Amazon. Pick a popular product, and use the browser Google Chrome Jungle Scout tool to see how much revenue the top sellers are pulling in. Success on Amazon is totally possible, and you need to have a positive attitude throughout the whole experience. There will be hard parts and things that might set you back, but you need to keep your head up and know that you will get through those hard times and succeed. You need to practice persistence and get words like "no" or "never" out of your head right now. Put all your energy into Amazon and implement your idea and product. Make your own luck. Put your business on multiple paths not just one, do everything you can to make it the best possible. Do what other people won't do. Do the hard work. Do all the extra marketing that others aren't putting in to make their product. This could mean putting in hours and hours into your Amazon business and not just one hour. Don't be afraid to make mistakes or fail the first time. Failing every once in awhile is how you learn and grow. Someday, pay your dues back to the community. Speak to the youth or a group of people about how you became who you are and created your business. This will remind you why you did this and give you motivation to keep pushing forward. During hard times, think about the good parts in your life - forcing your brain to remember a positive experience will give you hope. If you want to help your brain store positive experiences, reflect on what you are grateful for at least once a day. Professionals know that the more you hear a message, you're more likely to follow that message, right?

Repeat positive messages regarding your business and goals several times a day. Our brains actually make negativity appear to be worse than it really is. Try to distance yourself from negativity instead of dwelling on the past or negative things. Try listening to your favorite positive music and being around inspirational people. Make sure you are also still living life everyday and doing fun things, so you don't get overwhelmed by your Amazon business. There is such a thing as being unbalanced and working too hard, so make sure you are still sleeping, eating, and living life.

Each week, write down goals of what you will do to make your business better. Setting small weekly goals is great for measuring your progress, staying on the ball, and being motivated to succeed. Always look at the bright side of things. To practice being optimistic, think about what went that day before bed. Start your days focusing on goals and expectations, record your progress every day, be grateful, look for solutions first, and surround yourself with people that are this same way. You need to be committed to always learning and going beyond what others are willing to do. Follow everything we've talked about in this book. But, don't stop here. Continue to learn and research selling on Amazon. Keep your head swimming with great knowledge. I honestly wish every person reading this the best luck possible. Go beyond what others think is not humanly possible, and live a prosperous, happy life. Become one of the Amazon success stories and live the life you deserve.

Made in the USA
Lexington, KY
06 May 2018